Dog Groups

Hound Group

by Julie Murray

2

Dash!
LEVELED READERS
An Imprint of Abdo Zoom • abdobooks.com

2 Dash! LEVELED READERS

Level 1 – Beginning
Short and simple sentences with familiar words or patterns for children who are beginning to understand how letters and sounds go together.

Level 2 – Emerging
Longer words and sentences with more complex language patterns for readers who are practicing common words and letter sounds.

Level 3 – Transitional
More developed language and vocabulary for readers who are becoming more independent.

THIS BOOK CONTAINS RECYCLED MATERIALS

abdobooks.com

Published by Abdo Zoom, a division of ABDO, PO Box 398166, Minneapolis, Minnesota 55439.

Printed in the United States of America, North Mankato, Minnesota.
102023
012024

Photo Credits: Alamy, Getty Images, Shutterstock
Production Contributors: Jennie Forsberg, Grace Hansen
Design Contributors: Candice Keimig, Neil Klinepier

Library of Congress Control Number: 2023938002

Publisher's Cataloging in Publication Data

Names: Murray, Julie, author.
Title: Hound group / by Julie Murray
Description: Minneapolis, Minnesota : Abdo Zoom, 2024 | Series: Dog groups | Includes online resources and index.
Identifiers: ISBN 9781098284022 (lib. bdg.) | ISBN 9781098284749 (eBook) | ISBN 9781098285104 (Read-to-Me eBook)
Subjects: LCSH: Hounds--Juvenile literature. | Dog breeds--Juvenile literature. | Dogs--Juvenile literature. | Dogs--Behavior--Juvenile literature.
Classification: DDC 636.753--dc23

Table of Contents

Hound Group

The Hound Group contains more than 30 different dog **breeds**.

Rhodesian Ridgeback

Petit Basset Griffon Vendéen

The American Kennel Club (AKC) introduced the group in 1930. Dogs in the Hound Group were once a part of the Sporting Group.

Dachshund

The **breeds** of the Hound Group all look very different. They come in many sizes. But they were all **bred** to hunt.

Characteristics

English Foxhound

Dogs in the Hound Group hunt by sight or smell. Some use both senses.

Sighthounds hunt by keeping their **prey** in sight. They are fast runners!

Bloodhound

Scent hounds use their amazing sense of smell to hunt. They pick up scents on the ground or in the air.

Many dogs in the Hound Group have great **stamina**. They can track and hunt **prey** for long periods of time.

Greyhound

Beagle

Hound dogs can be difficult to train. This is because their **instinct** to hunt often takes over.

Some hound dogs make a unique noise. It is called **baying**. This sound lets others know they are pursuing their **prey**.

More Hound Breeds

Basenji

Ibizan Hound

Irish Wolfhound

Otterhound

Pharaoh Hound

Scottish Deerhound

Glossary

baying – barking with long, deep tones.

bred – developed over time for a certain purpose.

breed – a particular type of animal.

instinct – natural behavior in an animal that is not taught but is simply part of what the animal is born with.

prey – an animal that is hunted by another animal.

stamina – the strength to handle long effort.

Index

Online Resources

Booklinks
NONFICTION NETWORK
FREE! ONLINE NONFICTION RESOURCES

To learn more about the Hound Group, please visit **abdobooklinks.com** or scan this QR code. These links are routinely monitored and updated to provide the most current information available.